Lerner SPORTS

SPORTS VIPs

MEET
CONNOR
McDAVID

DAVID STABLER

Lerner Publications ◆ Minneapolis

Copyright © 2024 by Lerner Publishing Group, Inc.

All rights reserved. International copyright secured. No part of this book may be reproduced, stored in a retrieval system, or transmitted in any form or by any means—electronic, mechanical, photocopying, recording, or otherwise—without the prior written permission of Lerner Publishing Group, Inc., except for the inclusion of brief quotations in an acknowledged review.

Lerner Publications Company
An imprint of Lerner Publishing Group, Inc.
241 First Avenue North
Minneapolis, MN 55401 USA

For reading levels and more information, look up this title at www.lernerbooks.com.

Main body text set in Aptifer Slab LT Pro. Typeface provided by Linotype AG.

Editor: Annie Zheng **Photo Editor:** Nicole Berglund
Lerner team: Sue Marquis

Library of Congress Cataloging-in-Publication Data

Names: Stabler, David, author.
Title: Meet Connor McDavid : Edmonton Oilers superstar / David Stabler.
Description: Minneapolis, MN : Lerner Publications, [2024] | Series: Lerner sports. Sports VIPs | Includes bibliographical references and index. | Audience: Ages 7–11 years | Audience: Grades 4–6 | Summary: "Edmonton Oilers center Connor McDavid became team captain at the age of 19, setting an NHL record. Hockey fans will love learning about this star athlete's greatest moments, life off the ice, and more"— Provided by publisher.
Identifiers: LCCN 2023020727 (print) | LCCN 2023020728 (ebook) | ISBN 9798765624098 (lib. bdg.) | ISBN 9798765624111 (pbk.) | ISBN 9798765624135 (epub)
Subjects: LCSH: McDavid, Connor, 1997- —Juvenile literature. | Hockey players—Canada—Biography—Juvenile literature. | Edmonton Oilers (Hockey team)—History—Juvenile literature.
Classification: LCC GV848.5.M395 S83 2024 (print) | LCC GV848.5.M395 (ebook) | DDC 796.962092 [B]—dc23/eng/20230627

LC record available at https://lccn.loc.gov/2023020727
LC ebook record available at https://lccn.loc.gov/2023020728

Manufactured in the United States of America
1-1009642-51854-7/31/2023

TABLE OF CONTENTS

>>>>>>>>>>>>>>>>>

PLAYOFF HERO 4
FAST FACTS 5

CHAPTER 1
GROWING UP 8

CHAPTER 2
YOUNG STAR 13

CHAPTER 3
STORMING THE NHL 20

CHAPTER 4
THE NEXT ONE 25

CONNOR McDAVID CAREER STATS 28
GLOSSARY 29
SOURCE NOTES 30
LEARN MORE 31
INDEX 32

PLAYOFF HERO

The Edmonton Oilers had their backs against the wall. It was Game 5 of their 2022 playoff series against the Calgary Flames. The Oilers were down 4–3 in the second period. All they needed was one more victory to win the series.

The Oilers scored a goal to tie the game. Neither team could score in the third period. The game headed to overtime. Fans on both sides likely wondered the same thing. Who would step up and play the hero?

Five minutes into the overtime period, 25-year-old star center Connor McDavid answered the call for the Oilers. His teammate Leon Draisaitl picked up the puck near

FAST FACTS

DATE OF BIRTH: January 13, 1997
POSITION: center
LEAGUE: National Hockey League (NHL)

PROFESSIONAL HIGHLIGHTS: selected first overall in the 2015 NHL draft; named the NHL's Most Valuable Player (MVP) in 2017 and 2021; played six times in the NHL All-Star Game

PERSONAL HIGHLIGHTS: began playing hockey at the age of four; looked up to Sidney Crosby as a child; designed and built a home with his girlfriend, Lauren Kyle

Calgary's net. Draisaitl made a perfect pass to his captain, McDavid.

The Oilers captain shot the puck past the Flames goalie to win the game and the series. McDavid's goal sent the Oilers to the Western Conference Finals for the first time since 2006. Calgary's home arena burst into cheers. Many Oilers fans had made the three-hour trip from Edmonton, Alberta, Canada, to root for their team.

McDavid takes a shot at the net during Game 5 of the 2022 playoffs against the Calgary Flames.

The goal was McDavid's seventh goal of the 2022 playoffs. It was also the biggest goal of his NHL career so far. For seven seasons, McDavid had been one of the league's best young players. But now he added the title of playoffs hero to his name. The NHL's next Great One had arrived.

McDavid (*left*) celebrates after scoring the game-winning goal against the Calgary Flames.

CHAPTER 1

GROWING UP

Connor McDavid was born on January 13, 1997. He grew up in a town near Toronto, Ontario, Canada. His parents, Brian and Kelly McDavid, were both athletes who loved winter sports. His mother played hockey before she switched to skiing. His father also played hockey and grew up cheering for the Boston Bruins.

When he was three years old, Connor put on his first pair of skates. But they weren't ice skates. They were rollerblades. He spent hours skating around the family basement, shooting pucks at nets he had set up. He moved on to ice hockey after only a year. Before long, his parents could see he had a bright future in the sport.

McDavid attends the 2016 NHL Awards with his parents and brother. *Left to right*: Brian, Cameron, Connor, and Kelly McDavid.

Connor's parents encouraged him to play youth hockey. They could tell he was already far more skilled than other kids his age. But the local youth hockey team wouldn't allow Connor to play against older kids.

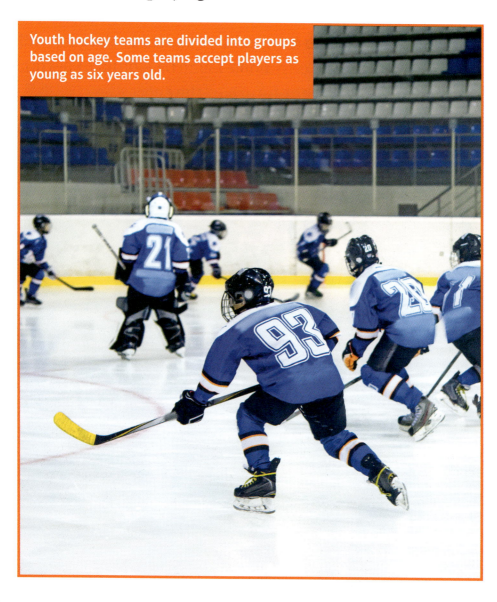

Youth hockey teams are divided into groups based on age. Some teams accept players as young as six years old.

SUPER SPORTS SCOOP

Toronto is the home of the NHL's Maple Leafs. But Connor's favorite player as a child was actually Pittsburgh Penguins star center Sidney Crosby.

So the McDavids signed him up for another team in a nearby town that let him play against older kids. By the time Connor was six, he was already competing against nine-year-olds. He ended up winning four titles with a youth team coached by his father.

Practice was a key part of Connor's success. He made sure he got on the ice every day. He even set up a practice course on his driveway.

He set up paint cans to rollerblade around. Sometimes he jumped over them. He set up a goal in the garage so he could practice shooting pucks into a net. Some of his wild shots even put holes in the walls.

Connor's skating reminded some of the great NHL player Bobby Orr. Others compared him to Pittsburgh Penguins center Sidney Crosby. Connor was so highly skilled that he received special permission to join the Ontario Hockey League a year early, at 15. Soon he'd be strapping on his skates and scoring goals for the Erie Otters.

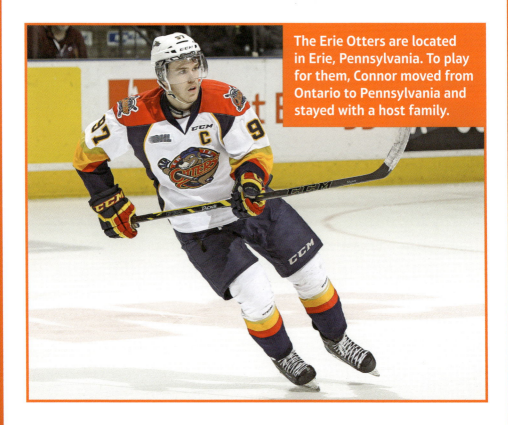

The Erie Otters are located in Erie, Pennsylvania. To play for them, Connor moved from Ontario to Pennsylvania and stayed with a host family.

CHAPTER 2

YOUNG STAR

Before his first season with the Erie Otters, Connor decided it was time to focus on his physical fitness. He teamed up with former NHL player Gary Roberts. Connor set a long-term goal of gaining 20 pounds (9 kg) of muscle. Together, he and Roberts came up with a diet and workout plan to help him achieve his goal. Connor and Roberts agreed to meet five mornings a week.

Gary Roberts warms up for a game against other former NHL players in 2017. He played in the league for 21 seasons.

"I was 15 and so nervous about meeting him," Connor said of Roberts. But he soon learned that Roberts was just another hockey fan with a passion for exercise. Their workout sessions paid off.

In his first season with the Otters, Connor won Rookie of the Year honors. "You build championships around players with this special ability," the Otters general manager said of Connor. "He's a very special person . . . to know him is to love him."

SUPER SPORTS SCOOP

In 2020, McDavid and Roberts created a fitness program to help fans stay active. These videos featured 15-minute workouts that people could do at home.

Connor (*center*) gets ready to snap the puck past the Niagara IceDogs goalie.

In his final year in the Ontario Hockey League, Connor became the Otters team captain. He scored 44 goals in the 2014 regular season. When he wasn't scoring goals himself, his passes helped his teammates score. He led the Otters into the playoffs, where he scored 21 goals in 20 games and earned MVP honors.

NHL teams began to take notice of McDavid's skills. He declared he would enter the 2015 NHL draft. McDavid expected to be the first overall pick in the draft, but he didn't know which team he would play for. A special system called the draft lottery would award one lucky team the right to pick McDavid.

McDavid holds the trophy for playoff MVP after the Ontario Hockey League championship final.

McDavid (*right*) receives his new jersey from Harrison Katz, son of Edmonton Oilers owner Daryl Katz.

At first, it looked as if the Toronto Maple Leafs might have a good chance to draft him. But the lottery winners turned out to be another Canadian team, the Edmonton Oilers. The team was coming off of a losing season and needed a strong scorer.

On June 26, 2015, the Oilers selected McDavid first overall in the NHL draft. Cheers rang out all over Western Canada as the young star pulled on his orange-and-blue Oilers sweater for the first time. "Now I'm an Edmonton Oiler. I couldn't be more proud," he said. "It's been a great day."

McDavid shakes hands with Daryl Katz after being selected in the draft.

CHAPTER 3

STORMING THE NHL

In July of 2015, Connor McDavid signed a three-year contract with the Edmonton Oilers worth $11.3 million. He played his first game on October 8, 2015. He scored his first goal with the team just five nights later.

About a month into the season, McDavid went down with a shoulder injury. He didn't play for three months. But McDavid still placed third for the NHL Rookie of the Year award.

In 2016, McDavid was named Oilers captain. At 19, he was the youngest team captain in NHL history. He scored his first hat trick in a win over the Dallas Stars a month into the season. Later, McDavid made his first All-Star team. He finished out the season as the league's top scorer and earned his first NHL MVP award.

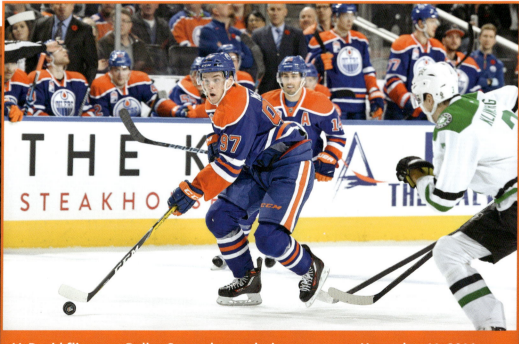

McDavid flies past Dallas Stars players during a game on November 11, 2016.

The Oilers also made it to the playoffs for the first time in 10 years. After the season, McDavid signed a $100 million contract to stay with the Oilers for another eight years. This makes him one of the highest-paid players in NHL history.

The next season, McDavid earned two more hat tricks and a four-goal game. But despite McDavid's leadership and scoring, the Oilers failed to make the playoffs in the 2017 and 2018 seasons. In the 2019 and 2020 seasons, they

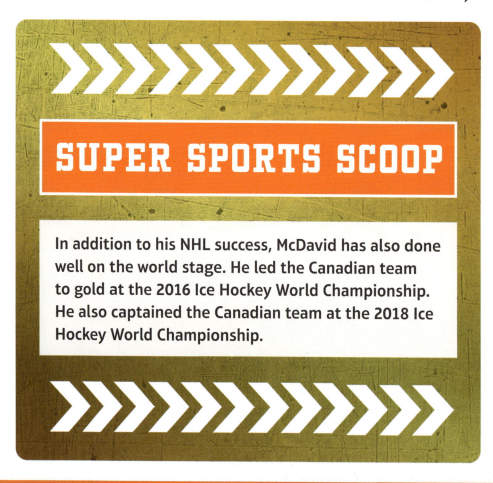

SUPER SPORTS SCOOP

In addition to his NHL success, McDavid has also done well on the world stage. He led the Canadian team to gold at the 2016 Ice Hockey World Championship. He also captained the Canadian team at the 2018 Ice Hockey World Championship.

McDavid swoops in from behind the goal to score in the third period of Game 7 against the Los Angeles Kings.

did make it to the playoffs, but they lost in the first round. Even though the Oilers didn't have success in the playoffs, McDavid still managed to earn another MVP title.

The next season was one of McDavid's best. He led the NHL in scoring. He also helped the Oilers become a top-ranked team going into the postseason.

The Oilers faced the Los Angeles Kings in round one of the playoffs. Down three games to two, it looked as if the Oilers might lose the series. But McDavid led his team to a comeback victory.

He recorded a goal and two assists in Game 6. He set up another assist and scored the game-winning goal in Game 7. The Oilers won the series.

Edmonton went on to defeat the Calgary Flames in round two. But they later lost to the Colorado Avalanche. Despite this, the team had come closer than ever to the Stanley Cup Finals.

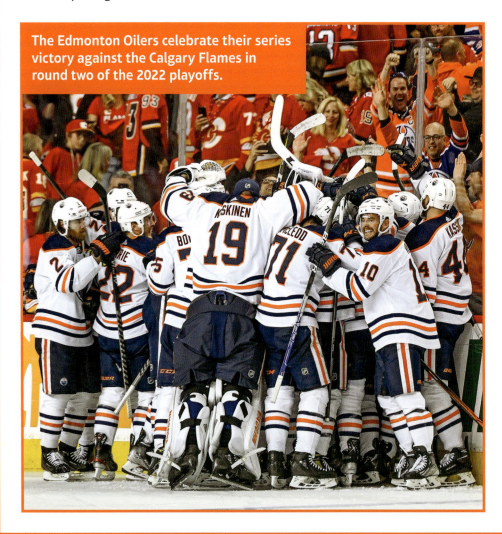

The Edmonton Oilers celebrate their series victory against the Calgary Flames in round two of the 2022 playoffs.

CHAPTER 4

THE NEXT ONE

After getting so close to winning a title in 2022, Connor McDavid had a tough act to follow. But his next season was even better. McDavid scored a hat trick on opening night against the Vancouver Canucks. This brought his total career points to 700. He is the sixth-fastest player to reach that mark in NHL history.

Ice sprays from his skates as McDavid attempts to score on Los Angeles Kings goalie Joonas Korpisalo.

The rest of the 2022–2023 season was filled with more milestones. McDavid scored 60 goals in a single season for the first time in his career. He finished the season with 64 goals and 153 points, the fourth most for any player in NHL history. The Canadian Broadcasting Corporation called it "the season of the century."

The Oilers finished second in their division and returned to the playoffs. They lost in six games to the Vegas Golden Knights in the second round. But despite this setback, the Oilers managed to leave their mark.

SUPER SPORTS SCOOP

McDavid's girlfriend, Lauren Kyle, is an interior designer. Together, the two designed and built their own house in Edmonton. They have their own sports court and even a heated driveway.

McDavid has already achieved so much at such a young age. Many hockey fans believe that he will one day surpass Wayne "the Great One" Gretzky as the greatest scorer in NHL history. But McDavid's biggest challenge will be leading his team to winning a title, something Gretzky did four times with the Oilers. If he does, McDavid will truly be the Next One in the eyes of hockey fans everywhere.

CONNOR McDAVID CAREER STATS

GAMES PLAYED:
569

GOALS:
303

ASSISTS:
547

POINTS:
850

Stats are accurate through the 2022-2023 NHL season.

GLOSSARY

assist: a pass from a teammate that leads directly to a goal

captain: a player who is the official leader of a team

hat trick: when a player scores three goals in one game

period: one of the divisions of playing time in a game. Hockey has three periods.

playoffs: a series of games played to decide a champion

point: a goal or an assist

pro: short for *professional*, taking part in an activity to make money

rookie: a first-year player

series: a number of games played between two teams

Stanley Cup Finals: the NHL's championship series

title: championship

SOURCE NOTES

14 Marty Klinkenberg, "How a Fitness Guru Helped Transform Hockey Prodigy Connor McDavid," *Globe and Mail* (Toronto), September 9, 2015, https://www.theglobeandmail.com/sports/hockey/how-a-fitness-guru-helped-transform-hockey-prodigy-connor-mcdavid/article26297428/.

15 Mike Johnston, "Otters' McDavid Named OHL Rookie of the Year," Sportsnet, April 4, 2013, https://www.sportsnet.ca/hockey/juniors/otters-mcdavid-named-ohl-rookie-of-the-year/.

19 Joanne Ireland, "Oilers GM Chiarelli Working on Tempering Expectations after Landing McDavid," *Edmonton Journal*, June 25, 2015, https://edmontonjournal.com/sports/hockey/happy-connor-mcdavid-day-oilers-to-make-no-1-pick-at-5-pm.

26 Jesse Campigotto, "Connor McDavid Is Having the Season of the Century," CBC, March 7, 2023, https://www.cbc.ca/sports/the-buzzer-newsletter-connor-mcdavid-2022-23-season-1.6771288.

LEARN MORE

Anderson, Josh. *G.O.A.T. Hockey Centers*. Minneapolis: Lerner Publications, 2024.

Bates, Greg. *Connor McDavid: Hockey Star*. Lake Elmo, MN: Focus Readers, 2019.

Kiddle: National Hockey League Facts for Kids
https://kids.kiddle.co/National_Hockey_League

National Hockey League
https://www.nhl.com/

Price, Karen. *Connor McDavid: Hockey Superstar*. Mendota Heights, MN: Press Box Books, 2019.

Sports Illustrated Kids: Hockey
https://www.sikids.com/hockey

INDEX

Calgary Flames, 4, 6, 24
Crosby, Sidney, 5, 11–12

Dallas Stars, 21
Draisaitl, Leon, 5–6

Edmonton Oilers, 4–6, 18–24, 26–27
Erie Otters, 12–13, 15–16

Los Angeles Kings, 23

Ontario Hockey League, 12, 16
Orr, Bobby, 12

Roberts, Gary, 13–15

Stanley Cup Finals, 24

Toronto Maple Leafs, 11, 18

Vancouver Canucks, 25
Vegas Golden Knights, 26

PHOTO ACKNOWLEDGMENTS

Image credits: AP Photo/Derik Hamilton, p. 4; Icon Sportswire/Getty Images, pp. 6, 20, 23, 24, 25; AP Photo/Larry MacDougal, p. 7; Claus Andersen/Getty Images, pp. 8, 12, 13, 17; Bruce Bennett/Getty Images, p. 9; Aleksandr Lupin/Shutterstock, p. 10; Andre Ringuette/Getty Images, p. 14; Vaughn Ridley/Getty Images, p. 16; Dave Sandford/Getty Images, pp. 18, 19; Andy Devlin/Getty Images, p. 21; AP Photo/Mark J. Terrill, p. 26. Design elements: The Hornbills Studio/Shutterstock.

Cover: AP Photo/Rick Scuteri.